CONVERSATION WITH MY FATHER WHOM I HAVE NEVER SEEN

CONVERSATION WITH MY FATHER WHOM I HAVE NEVER SEEN

Jessie M. Ruffin

iUniverse, Inc.
New York Bloomington Shanghai

CONVERSATION WITH MY FATHER WHOM I HAVE NEVER SEEN

Copyright © 2008 by Jessie M. Ruffin

All rights reserved. No part of this book may be used or reproduced by any means, graphic, electronic, or mechanical, including photocopying, recording, taping or by any information storage retrieval system without the written permission of the publisher except in the case of brief quotations embodied in critical articles and reviews.

iUniverse books may be ordered through booksellers or by contacting:

iUniverse
1663 Liberty Drive
Bloomington, IN 47403
www.iuniverse.com
1-800-Authors (1-800-288-4677)

Because of the dynamic nature of the Internet, any Web addresses or links contained in this book may have changed since publication and may no longer be valid.

The views expressed in this work are solely those of the author and do not necessarily reflect the views of the publisher, and the publisher hereby disclaims any responsibility for them.

ISBN: 978-0-595-48163-7 (pbk)
ISBN: 978-0-595-60257-5 (ebk)

Printed in the United States of America

Contents

SECTION 1: Understanding the Father and the World Through His Teachings 1

SECTION 2: Spirituality—A Defense Against Evil 6

SECTION 3: Love and The Father's Word 8

SECTION 4: Relating to Others 11

SECTION 5: Self-Development. 16

SECTION 6: Gifts from the Father 19

SECTION 7: Learning about the Father 21

SECTION 8: Love and Truth 23

SECTION 9: Faith. 26

SECTION 10: Helping Others through the Development of Self. 29

SECTION 11: Strength through the Father 31

SECTION 12: Understanding Others through the Father 34

SECTION 13: Purpose of Existing. 36

SECTION 14: Receiving the Holy Ghost. 38

SECTION 15: Being True to Ones Self 42

SECTION 16: Doing the Father's Will/Responsibility. 44

SECTION 17: Feelings 49

SECTION 18: Summary 54

SECTION 1:
Understanding the Father and the World Through His Teachings

My Father,

I have never seen You, but I know You are there and You love me. I have heard so many things about You, and read Your teachings. I have come to understand more of what and who You really are. As I get older and life goes on, I can understand that there are lots of things in life I will never know for reasons unknown. Father, it's not important that I know everything about You for to love You all I have to know is that you are in my heart. I don't have to accept who I am told is my father. That can cause all kinds of problems if in later years the question "Who is his real father?" is addressed. But I understand that at a certain age we know who is the "real" Father. I thank You, God, that I have experienced our salvational plan and I know beyond a shadow of a doubt that You are my heavenly Father.

I feel I know right from wrong and every person is created from the same source. Therefore, what is in me is in them; good or bad as it may be. I believe bad things come out of some of us because we do not know they are truly bad. Therefore, we feel we are not responsible for the evil we commit. Sometimes we have to be told what the bad things are in order to be helped. Also, I understand that I have to be told about some of the good that is in me in order for them to come out. Father, for me life is sometimes hard and doing what is right can be a struggle. But, I know I am not alone and You are here with me at all times. I must reverence You and call Your name for help. I know that is why You are always here. I understand that life is as good as one would make of it. Therefore, I can make what I want out of it as long as Your help and guidance are petitioned. That is why You gave me life in the beginning to learn about You and to give service, honor and glory to Your name.

Father, as a child I did some wrong things, but Your forgiveness was ever present and for this my heart will be forever grateful. I have never known anyone to love his children like You do. Through Your love for me, I now can feel the pain of other men and really care about them though I may not know what is going on inside them. I can now sometimes look at them and see the pain. I know it is through Your grace that I can truly look with an open mind and see the truth. I understand that I cannot be my brother or sister, but I can feel some of the things they may feel and go through. The thing for me to do is help them if I can in Your name. I know I cannot help them all, but by Your grace, Father, I can tell them what I know of You and hope they will want to know more. Father, I can remember bad days and good days, and now I see how both helped me to understand what You might be telling me if I only look and listen to what is going on with me in these times. The same holds true when relating to my brothers and sisters. I should not judge them since I do not know what is happening within them.

Father, I must stand for something knowing You will help me stand for that which I learn from You. Though I have never seen You, I feel a lot of you in me. I feel I can be the person You want me to be and live the **life** You want me to live. Mistakes I have made, many of them and will make many more I guess. But to learn from them is what I must do in order to prevent others from making the same mistakes. If I see what is happening to them, I will share my experience about that particular thing. I think I also understand that sometimes my mistakes have hurt others and I must try to make it right with the person(s) I have hurt in some way by being responsible for what I caused.

Father, I will always need Your help in my life because my life is unmanageable and many times I do not know what to do. Sometimes I long to have You touch me so I will know You are there for me. I am Your child, I have in my care some of Your other children and I am not there for them all the time; so I can understand how they may feel. However, I do love them and will try to help them understand that sometimes it may seem like I am not there for them, but like You, I am there inside always.

Father, I know people say "Like father, like son". I do have all that love in me, but unlike You, I do not know how to share it. I feel I cannot show everyone that I love them, so I pray to You so You can show them Your love.

Sometimes I feel like these are my children and I have to be responsible for them, but I cannot. I understand I have to only be responsible for me.

Father, I read in Your teachings that we all have the right to Your will or our own will. You gave us that and You will not take it back. I can turn my will back over to You if I am honest and true about it. Now I ask You, Father, to accept my will, I turn it over to You right now. For I feel that You know more about what I need than I do and how I can best help my brothers and sisters. For I only want to help. Father, let me help.

I feel that in this world there are two sides to everything. Men who understand and men who do not understand the difference in themselves or about the stillness of the world. I feel that we as men will never be together at all times on everything, but we can and should try to understand that we have one who is together on everything in this world. What does it matter who takes us down the right path as long as it is the right path (for me that is)? Father, I thank You for all I have learned and understood so far. Just like there is day and night for reasons unknown to me, I know and feel I will never understand all things for it is not meant.

Tell me what You want me to do and I will try to do it. Well, I know you want to know about me (smile). Right now I am feeling pain I have caused myself by doing the wrong thing for the wrong reasons. I have always felt the need to be around a woman most of the time beginning with my teenage years. I do not really know why, but I always found something wrong with them after a while; I was right because I would find out that they were also involved with one of my friends or someone I knew. But now I feel there could have been something in me that was not to their liking. As for boys and men, they always seem to think their girl or woman had a romantic interest in me or that I felt something and they could see it. So they would stay away until they wanted something from me. Most of the time they were right; I could have had relationships with their women. But, I did not while they were together. Well, this went on, as You know, for sometime. I could get money and most of what I thought I wanted and needed at that time. I was still lonely inside while living with some of those women. I thought I loved them and I did, but not in the right way. You know what I am trying to say, Father. At the time, I did not feel real. My thoughts were on things of the world.

I always wanted children, but did not know why. Now, I feel it was to keep me from being lonely. Well, I got married because the girl I was seeing was pregnant. So I came home from New York and got married; we had three children. Yes, I wanted children, but I did not know what it was to be responsible for them or whom it hurt when I was not responsible. Yes, I worked and put money in the house, but things still did not work out. I was working two jobs at that time. But, as You know, Father, I was drinking and doing things which had a lot to do with our problems; things got worse and worse at home. While on the road singing, I wanted to be home. So I went home one night without telling my wife and things were not any better with us; I left the next morning. Well, my job on the road ended shortly after we divorced.

I still loved my children very much. Although I did not show it often with money, I did give to them and visit them. As You know, I was blessed by You with more children when I thought I was in love; the relationship did not work.

Father, by this time I am older and still lonely inside. So You know what, I got married again. This time I felt the person was not in love with me, but that she was strong and would learn to love me because we did have fun together. She was smart and wanted what I wanted out of life. She knew I loved her; I was thinking, "Behind every good man, there is a better woman". Seeing what it meant to the other kids to have a dad around, I asked You to let me have another child (I did say son, I think) so I could make up for not being there all the time for my other children. I promised not to leave him; but I have, in a way, for the same reasons I did in the past. His mother and I could not live together; but, this time I was not having relationships with other women or drinking and it was not my doing. Still no excuse, Father, You and I know the whole story; You, more so than I, because You know the why and the what of it.

Father, I have learned to love my children more since I can talk to You person-to-person so to speak. My Father, I know not what to do. Please, help me once again for the child whose care You put in my hands is hurting and I can feel there pain. I do not know what to do about it. I know it might seem that I love him more than You, but You know that is not so. I guess I am trying to say, if I have caused him this pain, then let me suffer the pain or give my life for him. I am so very sorry this has happened to us all.

My Father, You know I wanted this marriage to work. Father, I feel I have learned something about what it takes for a marriage to work or just for people to live together in the same house or in a relationship. Both, I feel, have to like and love enough to respect each other's differences in any matter between both of them and be able to tolerate and endure what they do not like about the other person. Giving them the right to be the person they are. Father, I know that is hard for me to do sometimes, but I will try, Father.

SECTION 2:
Spirituality—A Defense Against Evil

I have never known anything about being a man as I see a man. But now, through Your grace, I am beginning to see what You meant for a man to be. I feel that the color of one's skin, his money, the possessions he has, or his works of life does not make him a man. It is the spiritual things inside of a man that make that man. I have learned if I am not spiritually connected with my Father, then I will miss all that is really for me. Father, I feel I have no identity and I am self-centered. Because of that, I am attempting to find out who and what I am and be comfortable with it. I cannot be what someone else wants me to be; I have to be me.

You know, I am learning that if I am spiritual, I can be more loving and kind each day that I see by Your grace. My Father, when I am, it feels good to give love to someone and not want anything in return. Sometimes the look on a person's face when You have helped them or shown them love where they thought there was none reminds me how good it feels to show love to someone else. Father, the feeling I get when I see a child with a happy face and the feeling from a child's hand holding mine while crossing the street; there is not but one thing greater than that feeling and that is feeling Your love. Oh Father, how I long to see You, to hear Your voice; I believe I will one day, for as real as You are in my heart, I know I will see and hear You. Sometimes I feel You so strongly in me that I just wish other people could also at the same time. With You I know that is a possibility.

Father, I do believe I should keep the focus on me in order to learn about me and what it is I should do. I have seen my brothers and sisters in trouble and pain because they do not know You or how to reach You. I have heard them talk about things they have done to one another and could not help doing them; they wanted to do better but could not, as though something had them. You know what that thing is and who, besides themselves, made them evil. I understand now that I nor anyone can fight it alone. We need You, my Father, and Your great benevolence. All of us who do not know that need to sincerely ask you and you will help.

I have heard my brothers testify that they have sexually had the sisters of other brothers they did not want to but did not have the power to do anything to stop it. I have heard them speak of the crazy things that go on in their minds, which I can testify to, for I have crazy thoughts in my own mind sometimes. But, now I know that I do not have to act on them.

I understand that there are suppose to be hard times and good times so I can learn from both and ask You, my Father, for help on the bad days and give You praise for the good days. I fear some of us do not know the meaning of this. For me, the good is coming from the spiritual part of me. I heard it said that the mind can do anything. Well, for me, it is in my heart because, Father, You are in my heart and I know without a doubt that there is no greater power. So, my mind is just there to let the good things and feelings out and show what they are. For me, if I am not putting anything out from the spirit (supernatural being) through the mind, then the mind is on its own and who knows what evil might enter and act out its will. Father, I feel we all have different ups and downs on different good and bad days. So somewhere in there we do feel and experience one another; therefore, we can learn from each other if we try.

SECTION 3:
Love and The Father's Word

Father, I understand that in You there is room for all Your children if we let Your will be done. I hear people say, "Well, you cannot love everyone", but I know the spirit that is deep within me does because You are here in me. I know I do not show it all the time and one might not know it to look at me, but You know. Father, I know every person has to ask forgiveness for him or herself and can if they choose to because we have a choice. I pray this prayer in the name of the Holy Spirit.

> I pray Father that we all would think about what you did for us, in giving up your only begotten Son out of love, just for the world.
>
> I pray that we love one another one step at a time each day of our lives. And I know you will help us accomplish that. Amen

Father, though I have never seen You, I know I will see You someday if I let what I feel for You guide my life.

My Father, I know You know what is in my heart at all times. Still, I hope it pleases You to hear me talk about what it is I feel. I am now just beginning to understand about older people, as we call them, and their memories of life. For them, in their times, the ups and downs, the good and bad, the happy or sad times, they needed to pray and knew not how or what to pray for. Father, I hope I can learn all of Your word and understand them and what I must do to always hear them. I wish sometimes that time for me would never end so I could always hear what You have to say to me in this life to keep me from sin. Yes, Father Whom I have never seen, I wish I could walk in Your Spirit that I might see and feel the very breath of Your love as surely as You did breathe it into me. And it is good to be here, though I am with sin; knowing that makes me realize how much I need You in my life each day of my life to help me be without so much sin and be forgiven when I am. I believe sin will be constant, but not like Your love—strong and everyday. Your will can keep me from sin, but nothing can keep You from loving Your children; no power of sin. None!

I can understand now why love is so much stronger than anything. For me, it is because the more I feel You in me, the more love I feel all over; that makes love come out of me abundantly. I never thought anyone could love so much, from the beginning to end until I begin reading about You. Father, that is You; loving from the start to the finish.

People say "You cannot love everyone, but after what I have learned about You and Your love, I feel we can love each other if we first love You and put that love in our spiritual being. Father, just let me awake each day in a spiritual way. I will love and act in that spiritual way. How can I love You or myself and not my brothers and sisters from within? Father, it is Your words that help me see how much I need to show love from within. It is Your love that I read about—the love for Your children and Your understanding of my imperfection; words that show me how to understand what You want me to do and how to be happy, joyful and free. I look around me and see how You made the earth so beautiful and know why we, as men, do not want to leave it; it is so easy to stay. All we have to do is let Your will be done. You said love one another and if we do, I believe there will be room enough for us all; if we all loved You enough to love each other, I believe we could stay. But, now only we who are chosen will remain.

I know that I'm not able to do anything if it wasn't for you Father. Thank You for having so much for me to learn about the world and my sister and brothers that are in it.

I wish my head could be in the right place at all times. But then, that would be like trying to be perfect and then I could not learn about anything or want to. Father, remember that day I was on the bus going downtown? You picked me up and showed me different people in all kinds of pain. Father thank you for allowing me to see the pain that my brothers and sisters were experiencing and I didn't have to endure that same pain. But still, I want to thank You for being there for me all the time. I just hope with faith that everyone in pain will feel the way I felt that day, very happy to know that You with Your mercy let me see that I did not have to live in pain anymore for any reason. All You do is good.

Father, let me always be in remembrance of that day, please. I saw how lucky I was to have someone as good and loving as You—a Father who knows all about me and loves me regardless. So, I ask You, my Father, to help me respect that love and remember that I asked to let Your will be done, not mine. I will at times want to take my will back, but I know that is not good. Father please keep me abiding in your word, and remind me not to pray so much for material things. You know I still like nice thing but help me to put you first in all things.

SECTION 4:
Relating to Others

I would like to help in some way and I know I have to be ready for that. Only You know when I am ready. We both know I like women a lot, but also that I know it only takes one. The right one and that is where I have the problem. Finding just one for a love match that is without payment; devotion to that person. I understand that there are all kinds of love and most of them I have tried in some way or another. Now, through prayer and faith in You, I will find the right woman for me (if it be Your will) and in Your time. Thank You, Father. I feel that there is a reason for me seeking the light at this time. If I have patience, I will come face-to-face with that which You have ready for me to do. I must have the courage to truly try to find my destiny. So I must stay in contact with You, my Father,

As You know, the relationship that I am in is not working. I think because the person and I are not into the same things now. Okay, I am trying to find out who and what I am and how I can help save my soul from sin and she is not into spiritual things and a lot of other things as I can see. But the thing now is that we are not married (as You know) but we are living together. I feel this is not the right relationship for me. I am feeling guilty about it and that tells me I need to do something about it. Please understand, as I know You do, that she is a good person, but like me and others she needs your help Father. I do pray for her daily. I really thought I had found the one for me, but I guess I have felt that way before. I have to look at all this as a learning experience.

I have come to understand that I do have a lot of anger in me, but talking to You is helping. My problem is that I let people "push my button" and I do not have to. I can have righteous anger. In any relationship both persons have the right to be happy or whatever, right'? To be honest, I like having things my way. Now I know that it should be what's best for the relationship. Yes, I have a lot to learn and I know the only way to get the true value and meaning of life is to have the ascendancy of the spirit. There is other help also: reading, people, particular places. But for me, all I have to believe in is the Word, the power of the Word, the beauty of the Word, and that the Word is.

Father, You must help me to know Thou will for I am willing. I know I have to go though a process. I think I am going through it now because I am willing to do anything to get ready to be used by you. I believe I can be, God fearing, loving, happy, joyful and free in mind and spirit. I am doing all I can to help. Father, keep me out of all the senseless things that I might have sanity to do the right things in all my goodness. Yes, I have to look inside of me and try to see what good is there and not be afraid to let it out. So I'm saying, know the good and not so good things in yourself so the not so good things will be easier to face. Now I can admit the truth about what I like and do not, knowing it might hurt someone's feeling. I can be comfortable with it because it is better to be truthful than in pain about what I really feel.

You know, Father, that I like women a lot, but they have to be partial with themselves about this or that, right! I use to be afraid to let them know what I did not care for in them for fear of hurting them. I did not like doing that, but I have learned through having some spirituality, that it is best to be true to one's self first. For example, if a woman's hair was not to my liking (long or short) or she was not clean in some ways, I did not say anything and it hurt me. All the good feelings that could have come out did not and yes, I know it is what is inside a person that counts. Okay. But for me, if you do not take care of yourself first, then that tells me something about the inside, you see. If there is spirituality in the inside, then it will show on the outside—no question! That is the way I see it. Father, if it sounds as if I want to be perfect, well, it can be Your will. From Your teaching, I understand that I can qualify to be most excellent in spirituality to Thee. Can that be good enough, Father? You gave me the skills and I am the one who has to work on them to create a more perfect union within myself and have faith that by Your grace, I can have a spiritual binding and reunion with You. So for me, my Father, I am asking You out of my soul and pray to You for wisdom so I can be wise enough to know that I need intelligence to acquire and retain knowledge and an understanding of how to go about being spiritual.

Yes, my Father, I will go on and on about what I have learned and how I have seen the pain in some men's eyes and felt the sadness in their hearts I know if they asked You out of their hearts that You would help them. I could go on and on about how I have seen a mother give a child her love and care and was happy doing it.

Oh, how sweet it is to know You, my Father, although I have never seen You. But I know I will one day. It is like I cannot see my feelings but I know they are inside and so are You. There is no substitute for You who gave a promise and a guarantee that You so loved the world. Father, if all men in the world would minister to each other in spirit and save one soul and that soul save another, we would all be okay.

We could then extend help to the children in the world so they would know at an early age that it is all about the inner spirit, saving souls, and understanding that it is not going to be easy. We go through things for a reason and we need to find out what that reason is so we can deal with it face-to-face, feeling there is help when we need it most. If we ask the right person, we will get the right help. These things I have learned from You, my Father, through Your words to me. If I am not or have no goals for what I want to be, how can any good things be seen by my children as an example? How can they see or have any idea of what they might want to be or what they want out of life? I have seen it so many times in kids; they did not know what they wanted to be. It is like walking. First, you let them know they are suppose to walk, then you show them how. When they see and understand what you are doing, in most cases, they are going to try it anyway.

I am learning about the spiritual energy in me. If I use that energy anything can happen. I have to find that energy and apply myself to useful things such as helping kids find the way to be happy, realize what they will get out of going to school, know which games are not fun to play, and understand things about life and how to live it in the soul as well as in the flesh. And yes, if I can love my spiritual self, I can love my brothers and sisters, love my neighbors, and not hate my enemies; We all need help in some area as people on earth.

Father, You know, right now I feel like I did when Uncle Willie died. I felt good all over, not sad. It was like You were telling me, "He is with Me and everything is alright". That is what was going on inside of me at that time. He was very real in my life; I did not know that until almost the end for him on earth, that he was important to me. You know, we would talk and laugh a lot when we saw each other. We enjoyed one another as two persons; he was a very good, spiritual person. His wife, Orene, and his son, Roger, have the same personality as Uncle Willie. Bless them, my Father, thank You.

There is another person with You who meant a lot to me. Different from the first, but still the same. They both meant a lot to me: my dad and Dookie, my stepdad. You know them both well. I told my dad how I loved him, but Dookie, I think he knew, we had very good times together when we saw each other also.

Father, that part of love I understand okay, but the love for a woman I have not gotten right yet. Now, I know it takes a lot of little things to do for a woman like holding her when you might not want to but you can see that she needs it or saying you love her a lot, going places you do not like with her. What I am trying to say is make her special in ways she would like and with things she likes—flowers, a little pat on the moon every once in a while, making her laugh, finding things to keep her happy, and then I will be happy. That is what I know about loving a woman and I am sure there is more, right?

I also understand that first I must be a whole person. For a long time I have known something was missing but did not know what until now. That is good for me because it is through You, my Father, pointing me in the right direction and putting things in my sight so I can see them and myself more. I now see that my main concern should be me and my being single first, to find out who and what I am. By Your grace, I will be all right with that. My whole self sound and complete in all things in general, a single unit. Father, You know what I am trying to say. Good, bad, and defects, all the things that make me a human being.

I have the understanding that with prayer and thanksgiving to You, Father Whom I have never seen, I can have a well balanced life, peace, and happiness. For if it were not for Your words that I read, these things I would not know. Father, is it not so that there are no two persons alike? Then I can be separate and unique in some areas of being a child of Yours, working on all of me as I need to come to terms with myself. Just to grow in areas of self is so good for me because I have never felt this way before. My God, I talk too much! Well anyway, it is nice to have someone to talk to anytime I want, anywhere I am, and about anything. I have so much to learn and now I'm willing to learn with an open mind and heart.

I also know that it will take time and patience and Your grace, my Father. You know, as I talk to You, I keep wondering when I will see You. Though I have never seen You, I will always be looking for You in every way I can and hoping a part of You is with me everyday I live. I know now that my life is nothing without You. Please be with me, Father, as I take this journey to be with You. Help me to use my time well and to help others, as I pass them on their way, to know You are the way.

I am truly glad to learn about thoughtfulness towards others, decency, goodwill, and things of that nature as part of my spirituality. Not to be perfect, but try to do as You have asked me to do. Now that I understand what that is, I know You would not have told me to take this trip if You were not coming with me, right? Yes, it is true, I am not in a hurry to get there; I will just take my time, if it is okay with You that is (smile).

SECTION 5:
Self-Development

I have so much to learn so I can grow inside and help someone. Father, just keep me in a spiritual way each day so someone will hear Your words and feel Your love through me, I pray.

Give me courage and willingness of thought to speak words of Your grace that might fill another's empty space. You know, I use to say "Why me?". Now I understand that I must go through some things I do not like, but I know they are required for me to know what I have gained by doing what is right and losing the pain of wrong doings at those times. Father, I can now see who is the head of this family and why You are. It began with You and it will end with You. I believe that in order to be in Your grace I have to let You be the head of my life. You gave me a choice and will love me whatever I choose. It is very clear to me what will happen if I forget about you. I know Your words are true. Everything I need to know is there and what is more important is that You are here also when I need help. If I do not get it, then I have no one to blame but me.

I now have control of my life thanks to You. By Your grace, I can now step out and try to really do what I would like to as far as being a whole person. Well, let us say in most things in my life I made the wrong choices. Now, You know, I am willing to do whatever it takes to get it together although I do not know what to do or how. I have faith in You now which I did not have before well, I did not know how it worked anyway. I now know, even if I were blind, I must try to walk forward and allow myself the chance to see from the other side. Father, You and only You know how I feel right now, I am alone in what I have to do, but not lonely. I am going to try to keep the focus of You on me so I can have a better relationship with You. Praying for Your will to be done and not mine. Asking that You take away all the crazy thinking in my head and let me know sanity. Father, Father, I look at my life and can see that I need a lot of help, okay. I still want to help other people so badly that I see or feel the need to help also. I know that is Your job unless You guide me to them. This has always been one of my "things", as we say. I see that I have to let go and work on me for if I am working on me, then maybe someone will see the change in me and be encouraged to follow me as I follow Christ. I understand the saying "Do unto other as you would have them do unto you". I will respect them and if they respect me, that is good. That is all I can ask from another person. I feel I have to keep my soul, my honesty, sincerity, and my spirituality growing.

Sometimes it is hard for another to see where you have grown and to what lengths you have gone to accomplish this growth if they did not know your weaknesses from the start. I am just beginning to grow as a man because I have stopped to look at life and me in it. Father show me what I need out of live and how to go about getting it. Thanks to You, Father, I can (by Your will) now lay down a foundation for the rest of my life to beginning with the basics. Knowing I have a loving Father who knows my heart and loves me, I must love my brothers and sisters and help them. They may not feel the same about me if they do not understand that, yes, some are in Your favor. By knowing our hearts You, my Father, can choose and have favorite ones to do Your work, but we know that You love us all the same. I say instead of looking at John and saying "Old John thinks he is something", we should look at John's heart and see why he is in Your favor and try to seek those things that would put us too in Your favor. I believe if I look for the good in one's heart, then the scars on the outside should not matter. My foundation will be built on love and helping my brother find his Father, for I have found Him and He will be the same one; this I do know. My foundation will be to find the reason why my Father cannot be here with me so I can see Him. This foundation will take some time I understand because it will need a lot of help. Who will help? To have a good foundation I need good supporters, Father. You know my heart, so please find favor in me and give me Your support.

Father, today I saw a lonely man. I saw in his eyes that he was looking for someone but did not know how to seek You and knowing that in You he would never have to be lonely again in life. So not knowing, he turned to drink; I saw the sadness running down his body and how it hurt him to do that. It was in his face and yes, it reminded me of someone we both know. I saw no foundation of love, morals, or respect for himself. No courage, no discipline, no confidence or willingness to endure hardship of his self-willed mind. My Father, I pray, please take away my self-will and let Your will be done. Okay? I know not what to do, but through You, Father, if You will, please help me to be of help to persons such as this for Your glory not mine.

I remember once in my life trying to carry myself in a righteous manner at all times. People would say I was too righteous; I did not know what they meant. But now, I understand that I was only trying to be right-minded; thinking or believing what is righteousness to me. So for me, all I do good is glory to You for it is because of You, not me, that I can do good. I see that person I was and still am. Now, some of me can and will be changed by Your grace because I am willing to look at all of me and go on trying to be better. Not knowing what was wrong was like looking for attention in the wrong way for myself. I need to know why I did such things as dressing well to make me feel good about me. That might be okay, but I know that I do not need that now. I feel I have to give up the pain of not being successful when I think I should have been and deal with where I am, making plans for where I would like to go. Father, someone asked me how I could believe so much in a Father Whom I have never seen and I replied, "How do you know when you have drank a cup of water?"

SECTION 6:
Gifts from the Father

It is said that You gave all Your children a gift and I believe that. I have to focus on my many gifts, thank God. The gifts of love and happiness are mine and yours too, okay? In learning about things, Father, I believe You want me to be happy so You can be happy also in all of Your children. To see us adjust, come into a clear image of ourselves and meet it actively, and reflect honor on You, my Father, is great, great, great!!!

My Father Whom I have never seen, I love You and need You to be right where You are in my life. I know You are here with me for always and things will be okay for me. Father, I believe I have felt You smile and felt your presence for me as I had to do or not do something for my son, Marcus, own good. The feeling of power from You cannot be described. That is how close You are at times. Regarding the powers in me, sometimes I have, as You know, difficulty displaying them and getting them to come out as I feel they should. I mean in serious events, it is like thinking with my heart and not my mind. When I am thinking with my heart, it always turns out right. I do not know why, Father, but it seems I have more energy of feeling for my belief of the right things, but I can and probably will do wrong sometimes. That is why I need Your will to be and not mine. Sometimes it seems that it takes so much energy to live in this world, but then I have to remember that You are here to help in matters of indecision. I do not know why it is so hard for me to make up my mind about a lot of things. I guess I want to be right so badly that I am afraid of being wrong, or to face not being right as I see it. Now I see, Father, is when I can have faith and confidence; to be sure of myself is good for me.

Father, I have been asked to be a Trustee or Deacon in church and I am asking for Your help in this. Give me strength and understanding with awareness so I can do a good job. Help me have the wisdom to follow the soundest course of action and use good judgement in all that I may do. Oh Father, keep me teachable. Give me patience to let Your will be done. Help me seek Thee in spite of the things of the world.

SECTION 7:
Learning about the Father

Education can do a lot in helping develop my mind and knowledge in lots of things; not just for me, but for us all. To learn from one another is a good thing. That is my belief. Father, talking to You sure gives me the incentive to act on some good goals. Just to keep this motivation, I guess I will have to keep talking to You and hearing what You say to me. For I know I could never have a better relationship with anyone. I believe that surely, goodness, and mercy shall follow me all the days of the rest of my life because You, my Father Whom I have never seen, are with me. If I could talk to other people in the way I talk to You, I am sure I could help someone in need of knowing who You are and that You will do for them also, as You have helped me. After all, we are all Your children.

I know it is hard for someone who does not know You or have a relationship with You to believe in all they hear people say You can do. I guess a person has to have something very good happen to them to look up and say, "Thank You", and believe that You, Father, were the only one who could have allowed such a good thing happen to them under the circumstances. When people are in distress and come out, they know that God was the only one who could bring them out. It is my belief that if they are good inside, something will happen to let them know You are real and are there for them. I believe some of us have to be all the things we are not in order to be all the things we are so the glory can be given to You, my Father, with understanding that had it not been for You there would not be anything to want, touch, feel, see, hear, love, dislike, be happy about or enjoy. Many more things are better in Your world, I know we all will see this and stay in Your world with You. I will try to help anyone I can to come, if it be Your will. I only want to be aware of the vision You give to me for Your will to be done, and that my brothers and sisters will know this and give You their love. I would like to see the children get to know You, so when they are grown they will know it is by Your grace and love that You have something for them to do with Your will.

Based on what I have seen I do not believe we can tell children they can be anything that they want to be, not before they know that all good things are given by You. If it is not a good thing that they wish to be, then yes, there will be a price to pay. That is the way I feel about it, Father. I understand that You can take away anything You give, but we as persons can also give and take. If we do the wrong thing for the wrong reason it can cause us our lives. Please give me strength to do Your will with perfection and consistency. I am beginning to like myself more just by learning about You and Your ways of life for me. One of the things You would have me do is bring Your love into the open so all can see and know who holds the power of the truth.

SECTION 8:
Love and Truth

For me love is true and truth is love. Men will say "I love the game" and that means they will be true in what they have to do in order to get to play it. They are so close and so strong, not like some men—weak. True love is always strong and all I have to do is look at what You did with love. You gave Your only begotten Son and look how truthful He is; so much so that He said He would take me back and I believe Him. That is true and unconditional love for me, my Father. I will try to love You with all the true love that is in me.

Father, why does man duplicate the things of this world and not you, but I know not one trying to duplicate Your love of him or the things of. Could it be that he has not learned how it works. My Father Whom I have never seen, You know how I long to be with Thee and long for my brothers and sisters to know the power of love and truth. I guess that is Your will too. I know, I should stop worrying and leave the world to You. Right? Right, I will try.

Father, You know, today at work the doctor told me a lady was going to die and he could not save her, but he would tell her that she has two months to live. He then asked me if I thought he should give her that time and I said, "You know what? I felt I knew You, Father, could save her. I wanted You to do it through me to show Your power and get the glory. But then, she should know it was You and give You the praise. Why was this my feeling, my Father? Oh, I forgot, things are better done Your way because that is the best way and everyone involved benefits when things are done Your way.

Father, help me be the person on the outside that I am on the inside. Most of the time I feel in touch with what is inward. For instance, let us say a woman I am seeing tells me she is not involved with a man that I see her with and she says she is not with him. In my heart, I take up *for* her because I want to trust her. But I do not know why I *feel* that way inside *for* her and others as well. It is as if I hope they will do what is best for them. I want to understand everyone's feelings and try to excuse their actions. You know what I am saying. I love them on the inside, but I cannot let it out in a way in which they will know. I have just learned the difference between what is best for me and what is in my head. Now I know the things in my heart are true. I did not know how to tell the difference until now. I can basically go on what is in my heart rather than what in my mind.

I always reach out in my heart, but not often with my actions or words so people will know just how I feel. Help me with this, my Father. For you know the complete person inside and out. I believe in listening to You with my heart; the person I would like to be will emerge by Your grace and love, my Father. I can see that I need to talk more about who I am to determine if I really am that person inside; sometimes I do not know. I think I let the things people say effect me a lot. I can say you know because You really do.

I was reading Your words the other day and was surprised at how much I learned and understood from within about what You were saying, my Father. I hope all will feel Your presence in time to come and life will change for the good of all of us. We must get into you for you are already in us.

I believe to be holy would be happiness for me—to feel that saintly spirit without deceit or fraud, upright and sincere. Holy! Holy! The true way of life, that is what I am looking for and why I am looking for You, my Father. I believe I know the true way of life and what I must do to live that life—to give You what is Yours and that is me. I believe You will let me have the desires of my heart not my mind; things that are pure and true to my life in You not the world. Right now my desires are to try and be in You more than anything and learn all I can of Your will for me. I want to learn how to let it be done, to love myself more so I can love others more, and judge not lest I judge myself. Let me show love to my brothers and sisters in the outside world that the glory of You may be seen; to help just one person see Your greatness as often as I can. With You as the head of my life, how happy my life can he.

I desire to work on the not-so-good things about me to become whole within myself. I do not know how right I can be, but I have a desire to be as right as I can, as often as I can, about all that I can. That desire is in me, but if and when I am not right, then let that desire be gone. You know what I am saying, Father? In me is the desire to fix all things if I can. You know, it is a true desire of mine and I believe it to be a desire of hope that You are going to help me obtain because I know You can.

The utmost I desire from my heart, Father, is to one day be with You and at the same time be in love with you. I believe the feelings in me will change as I grow in spirit and in holiness by Your grace. My desires will be better for in holiness all things change for the better. I have put my trust in You and I know I must now do that which I know and believe is right. If not, then how can I expect You to keep Your word and help me in Your word?

Father, my desire is to be one of those whom You will be in the midst of You know, as I talk to You and read Your words, I can feel myself really growing up. Not like when I was a child—I just looked and one day I was not a child anymore. Now I have that "eyeful" view which I understand better because I am more complete in what I see. My range of knowledge is broader than when growing up. Yes, there is pain, but I now know how to handle it. All I have to do is ask for Your help, Father. I know You are not so far away after all. It is strange to know the feeling of not having problems awaiting you when you get up in the morning although what that day holds is unknown. Just the feeling of knowing that day is coming is so good (Glory!). Surrendering myself to trust in one greater than I is joy in itself and that someone is You, Father.

SECTION 9:
Faith

I hear men talk of faith in different ways. Some say there is more than one kind of faith with different meanings. There are types of faith that can be what we want them to be. How can I say I love You and believe in what You teach as truth and not see through faith that you can do all things. When I read about You, though I have never seen You, I hear You talk to me. I believe what You say even when I do not understand what You are saying. I hear the truth in Your words as if You were in front of me. I hear a perfect voice with real feeling. I know You have given me a foundation for life and if I do not believe, You will not force me to believe because that is not Your purpose. When I was given the gift of life, the element of faith was there because all things exists. How can I hope for something I do not believe exist?

    I can see now why some men do not know the purpose of their lives. It is because they have not made anything out of it, so there is no reason given for the gift. This, Father, You know more about than I. You forgive and so do I because You are in me; therefore, I try to let things men do to me or things I do not like pass with forgiveness. You know how much I struggle with the way things are going in the world—boys killing boys and girls; just hating each other it seems, I cannot understand it. At one time, it did not seem to matter until I began to change my life through Your grace. I guess it was there down inside of me all the time. Now that it is out, I feel the pain of it, the caring and I know You will take care of it. It is so hard to have a great deal of faith in what I do not see, so I guess I will continue with this little bit I have until it grows with prayer.

    I am glad I understand why men cannot give me a parable of truth to any promise they make because they do not have that grace in them of faith to be a mentor. Father, just think, if I did not have this personal relationship with You.

I would have to depend on man's attitude toward You. That would be unfortunate because of his strong desire to focus on what he can and cannot do.

I always thought I was suppose to be a Christian. If I can just be saintly I can be a good Christian—believing in faith, love, spirituality and truth is what I am trying to say. Father, I really need Your help in what I am about to take on.

I need You with me because without You this will not work. I only know one way to do it and that is to have faith in You—that blind faith in things not seen for I know You can work it out for the best. I know going into this, something about it is wrong but I believe in You and that You will help me get those things right. I pray that You will answer my prayer for I will be praying. This is a substance of things hoped for with no evidence, You know. But, I will be listening for Your words. I believe I will hear them; I will understand and obey. I can say I know this is not something I truly have to have, but in all reality would like just for me in that I have that choice given to me. Also for me, it shows how my life is unmanageable without You in it; the truth is, it is a man's thing. However, man cannot help me—only You and Your grace.

I suppose this is a time of dreams for me but not of my mind or sleep. In my heart images of real love and freedom from war with the adversary, who sometimes I may not know by name or face or image, place me in a position where I must stand with You, my Father; yet I have never seen You. I know You are the only one who can see my heart and dreams within, hoping they will surface. Oh how I love You and wish to know You better. I believe all that is in my heart which is good and true is of You. Father, help me for I know not what I do. Right now, only You know that I am the little boy who always dreamed of holding his father's hand while going places and now awake to find his father is not there; feeling without his father's guidance, he would not make it. Yes, right now I feel that way. But I am going to do the only thing I can and that is turn it over to You, my Father. I pray You will make me inherent of being strong for I will need it. I will know tension and stress in this difficult relationship, but I believe with Your help, it will not be impossible to turn around. With You all things are feasible and more. I know this because there are some things I do not like doing on and off the job but now that I am trying to stay in more of a holy spirit, it is better most days and I know that is not my doing. Okay? For prayer and praise, I thank You, my

Father. I hope it continues because it feels good to be good or act kindly; it just does. I hope, everyone has had that feeling or will.

Oh, since I am felling so honest about things right now, I will tell You about the job I have now. Yes, I feel I should only do things on my job that are in my job which is Ortho Tech work Nursing service wants me to do nursing assist work in addition to my other work without additional pay; I really do not like that. So please help me with this for I do need a job! Sometimes I am hesitant in doing things I should do, but I must press. I know. But, I must press on. Again, I need your; Help!

SECTION 10:
Helping Others through the Development of Self

There are some people I do not like, but I really get along with most anyone, as You know; I hate no one. However, some people sure make it hard sometimes not to dislike them. So, I pray on it. My Father, I am finding it easy to be honest when talking to You and feel free and real; this is good. When I read Your words, I have that same free feeling and joy. Father, how is it that some things need to change and do not, then others should not but do so? As it is said, man was born in the spirit of God, one is flawless and the other is not. How can I gain this representation of my likeness though born in sin and yet be saved from sin, but will never be perfect except by Your grace? I do believe that one day I will be perfect enough to be with You, My Father, and have all the answers for there will be no problems.

Right now, I have to work *on me and* myself; things to do and not to do; to live right for I know that I cannot have the feeling of inner-peace if I am not living in a righteous way. I hope to grasp more of You and Your word each time we talk or whenever I read Your word. Your being with me makes me happier than ever. Yes, I know being here in this world, I will get hooked on some of the things in the world—for me it is clothes and You know, I like clothes. Some doctors say that if looking good makes you feel good, then do it. Let me tell you, not so all the time, okay. Sometimes I look like a "mill" but feel like you-know-what. I guess because coming up we were poor (so I thought then). If only I knew. I said to myself I will never be without clothes again—that might be one reason, but I thank You for them. Thank You, my Father. That is just one of the things I am going through and You know the others. We will talk about them another time, my Father.

I feel it is hard to live up to an image you have been given not knowing the pureness of that image. You know what I am trying to say; I feel I must seek

You to know the innocence of myself. I was talking to an older man today and he said he hated being old and that he was becoming more like a baby again. But what I heard him say out of innocence was that he dislikes the way in which he is becoming old; he blames You, my Father. But I knew You had nothing to do with the way he was getting old for I think the way he or she grows old is his/her own fault.

If I treat my body right and do the right things I pray for the body and meditate on body exercise and things of that nature. I can and will thank You for letting me get old and not blame You for the way I walk or talk at age 60 or more. You know, the older I get the more I can learn and see Your works; the more I learn the more I can help someone else. I believe I am just beginning to become a man for I am now learning of You and Your will for me. I believe males cannot be whole until they are in You, with You, for You.

I felt sorry for that man, because I could see inside him. It seems he just did not know how to live. Only believe—that is my desire for all men now. Just let the desires of thy soul be known to thyself and pray to make them right in thy heart. Father, the way I feel about You now, I know if You ask or tell me not to do something I would obey. I hope to get in the habit of doing things as right as I can in the beginning, in whatever I do, my Father Whom I have never seen. I will try to speak of You everyday to as many of Your other children as is allowed.

SECTION 11:
Strength through the Father

Right now, my mind is going back to my new relationship with a wife. Father, even as I am talking to You, I think I know now how to be a good husband and friend to a wife. I understand why she is the weaker one. As for me, I am the weaker. She needs me to be a man and help her. I need You as a Father to confide in. I see that if I put her first she will help me. As a result, I will receive things a woman give a man in spirit mind and soul. Therefore, we will pray and put you first in all that we do. You will give me what I need to give life to her and the fruits of 'my hearts desire. I now see how marriage is to work for both persons. Being single the wrong way inside, I truly did not know what putting your wife first meant until now just by having this conversation with You. It is as if You are sitting right in front of me explaining everything to me. I can see it, I can. It is evident that anyone who is a part of what makes life work for them is significant. I know this by seeing how important You are in my being and life. I clearly take the blame for my other relationships and marriages not working. I did not assume my God-given appointed role as head of the family. I think I have always had a bad communication problem, I guess because I never took the lead even when I knew I should. But now, I feel I have a better understanding of my life and how it should be with me in You.

I think I can be strong and use the strength You gave to me. For instance, today I saw three men with different handicaps and I could see each ones personal problem with that handicap. I felt the way each of them felt just looking at them and not their handicap. I said, "Praise the Lord!", being thankful it was not me and yet, not sorry for them. I had strength to look deep inside me and then to feel. ThankYou, my Father, thank You. And so, what I am feeling is that a woman is to look for strength from her man. Is this not so, my Father? I did not know that as a man much is dependent on you by the female, so many things. That is okay, for is this not why You made her this way out of man—to receive or acquire just as man was made in Your own image to be Holy, spiritual, kind, loving, and so on?

My Father, every time I start talking about You and love, I see a reflection of peace—I do. I could walk around with it forever. Yes, I know I am in the world so it will not be easy. I care. So, if I care, then I must suffer something. I do understand, Father.

More questions, Sir. Why is it some people seem to put things together when it counts and others do not? Well, You know what I am saying and of whom I speak—my American black brothers and sisters. We just do not seem to get it—love for each other, that is. Yes, whites dislike each other and other groups, but they all come together as a whole when it counts. It is not a lot of killing one another over small things like mother or daddy not doing or giving them this or that, hating them for being sick in their time of bringing them up. If you were mistreated then but now are grown, then I feel you should know that somewhere in your family line there was a problem. If you are not being treated right, then know there is a problem and if there is a problem, there is an answer. The one who has the answer is waiting for you to ask for help.

I know we can do better for ourselves if we try to respect each other and each other's differences of opinion if only long enough for it to count as a whole in our race. Why is it that we say they are the cause of this and that and not look at ourselves and see how so many can be so weak? We were made strong. And in reference to our history, we have been with the top in all things from *the* beginning. Why not now, Father? Is it not time for Your help in the whole matter? We are the cause of our own shortcomings as a black breed of people.

And yes, I know it is not about the world or the brothers and sisters of color, but the message we each get for ourselves. I guess it is like the song says, "Some of us will and some of us won't". Some can and some cannot understand the whole picture. But, I had to ask. For I know You, my Father Whom I have never seen, are the source and resource that we need to seek in all of our lives. You are for me anyway.

Father, it seems I hurt with a lot of feelings not of my own. What is this I feel? Why in this moment while talking to You—this feeling of love and wanting to do something for all, why Father? Can love make you do right? I think so. For if you love from deep within I feel you will do right because of that feeling eating away at you like it has a mind of its own.

My Father, I have found that I have an intelligence of heart as well as of mind; information is also there. Within waiting, that intellectual part of me, the soundness of soul is so great; this quality of ones self. Now that I realize the power You have stored in me, how can I not love You, Father, for I have all l need and more. I have You, my Father, who will never be past, but always current. I hope to stay more curious about my spiritual being than all my worldly saying concerning the church, my Father. Why is it that some use it for other things that are not of the church or its matters? Is it because we are weak at heart or just do not love You enough? I am sure it is both. The things that are done in your churches are not always of you. Father thank you for forgiving them. How great Thou art!!!

I guess with so much love for Your children, how can You not forgive those who do not know any better in their minds and hearts? I see that with all the love in You this is just a little part of it. Father help me forgive things also when they happen. For You know that I do, but it sometimes takes me a while. Only after I have thought about it, then I forgive all. I feel that forgiving should come automatically if you love one another. Right? Just my opinion. That is okay, for now I see it all as just about love for each other and to have it, one must give it. The way I treat you says more than what I say in most cases concerning love, I think. I can say I love you over and over everyday—just words. But when I hold you and say it, how different. Try it on someone and you will see. What I am saying, Father is I see what a powerful feeling love is. I see that what You did with it. I can imagine You looking down into that feeling and making something out of it. My Father, cannot we, as Your children, do the same? Look into love and make something good out of it. Why cannot we embrace with an attitude this powerful gift that is being given so freely. Thanks to You, my Father Whom l have never seen, I am beginning to have a personal attitude about things and want to know the answers. So I must come to You, Father, for these answers.

SECTION 12:
Understanding Others through the Father

Oh yes, Father, concerning things about You that man does not know or understand but want to know because men of science and religion are in disbelief of You and Your origin. There are still some who, like me, know You are real in life and in the universe. Some would like to prove that it is something other than You, my Father, that doth all things in order. They say there are other reasons for things in the universe. Some seem to think there is a source of matter and energy that they can catch onto in some way and control, that is what some of the writings I have read indicate, My belief, of course, is that there is a purpose in the universe as is in all things. That only means that we have to see the one who is all things to know the meaning of these things. If I am of love and I want you to love me, then I must do something to make you come for that love. So, I show you love and let you feel it and you will want it for it can be like that house you saw or that car you saw and wanted. But first, what is the source of my desires for these things.

After seeing them and wanting them, I cannot just go and get them, can I? I think not. I have to go to the person or persons who are the owners or makers. Let us just say the creator of these things. Right? You would then pay the price for that which you want. But to find out why, who, and where all things and I came, all I need do is seek You, my Father Whom I have never seen, and You will know the answers to the beginning. For in my heart, I have faith in things not seen but hoped for and I know where that hope lies—it lies in You, my Father.

I cannot make matter or energy because they are already made and out of those two come other things, in my opinion, Father. You said talk and You would listen and I have been talking. I guess just being able to talk to You at this time all my thoughts are here at once. You know my life has been so down; as I see it, until now that I have found You, Father. You have always been with me; if only I had known. It does not matter who or what I am, be it just a cell or an organism, or what all of these things people and scientist say. I keep remembering it was said, "in the beginning there was …" Right? I believe science will give us the proof of the greater power and only power, not that there is not a power. I feel like I am taking flight like a bird up, up, and away. But, it is in my heart, a free swift movement. It feels like the air is sweet, not a sweet smell. Strange it is, but the spirit of it is good.

You know, Father, I wonder sometimes why I cannot fly. The birds look so graceful and at peace in flight; and oh so happy as though playing with You. Sometimes I feel You are having fun and I hope that one day we will play together.

I will try to keep my heart free from resentful thoughts. It is hard to do some of the time with my brothers and sisters. I guess I just have to look at the world from the inside, if that can be done. I believe it can be done for it too has a heart—the heart of its origin. I must look at that because that is what is true. The things that are in the heart of the world that I must find to live the righteous way in the world as I am learning from You, my Father. Father, I hear You breathing as though You were here and my head was on Your chest and Your arms around me; so cool and warm. All is at peace in this moment.

I understand now, that I will have to keep goodwill toward my brothers and sisters at all times, if I can, in order to be free outside of them. Yet, I cannot carry the pain of them though I feel it or the thoughts of them. I am thinking of them; I cannot carry them. I have to keep admitting and remembering that I am powerless over them.

SECTION 13:
Purpose of Existing

Father, now that I know where You are and that I can talk to You at anytime, I ask You to help me change to be a better person; the person I would like to be in You. What is it You want me to do, Father? Tell me and I will do it. I am willing to go through whatever it takes because I know You will be with me. I ask You to bless all the people that I pray for each day as I have been doing for sometime now, but You know this. Please bless them, my Father. Help them find their real Father as I have. Let them know he loves them as he loves me. Help them in their hearts that they understand that all they need and desire is within them, for You are in them.

Yes, Father, I would indeed like to know my purpose here or should I say Your purpose for letting me be here. I understand that I can give myself a purpose by You giving me a choice in the matter, but it would not be real, that is the way I feel about it. Some of us know our place in life right away—what You want us to do—but I do not; I want very much to know what it is I am to do. I believe there is something I can do for You, Father, though I have never seen You.

I know there is something. Just to live a good life is not enough. To be happy, joyful and free, that is for me. But, what about You, Father? You know, sometimes I get depressed because I cannot do anything, yet I know all things of You are done in Your time, Yet, I am sad. I guess I just need You to talk to me sometimes to let me know what to do. I hear my brothers and sisters say, "Get into the word and what it means". It is a lot to learn and know how to use it correctly. But, I will do it in some way with the help of my inner spirit, of course, for I believe in the word—Your word. Yet, I might hear them through another, but if I know the word, then I will know from which they came.

Father, I know I am just talking on and on from one thing to another, but these are the matters in my heart (as You know). Besides, it gives me a chance to say, "I love You, Lord", while I know You are listening. You know, a lot of people ask if I am a minister or why I am not one. I wonder about that myself, but I have never thought of being a minister or one to give religious services until now, and only as I talk to You, Father. I would just like to get to be in You at all times, well most of the time, and at peace with me. You know? You say I can, so I guess I will be, right?

Still there are so many people I would like to help. Look at me, I cannot help myself right now. But, by Your grace I will. Yes, I believe I will try and have a little song in my heart and live right about now. A little joy can never hurt a man in the world, yet it is so far from me in times like this. I know—keep the focus on You for I cannot do anything for the people as a whole, as for changing them and their evaluation of treatment of one another. So, if I help me, then maybe some looking at me can see something that might help them to change something in their life. We have to change a lot of our inner-self to make it work on the outside and in the world, my Father. I feel that if I were in Your favor, You would give me at least one wish, I would wish that You would give us more time to learn how to let Your will be done and let You work out our problems for us. For so many of us do not know how great You are and that You truly love us. I wish time would stand still long enough for one of us to see and know the real truth. There is a place in us with peace and love waiting to come forth, but I guess I am dreaming for You have the answers to all I want to know about. Now, I am sad again because I know it is not alright for some of us and I can do nothing about it but let it go.

SECTION 14:
Receiving the Holy Ghost

Father, I am made in Your own image, yet out of the same image as my brothers and sisters; good and bad. So I cannot be that perfect person for You and I am sorry, Father, for I love my brothers and sisters, too. Yes, some more than others. However, they all are loved in me and welcomed. Yes, l know I sound a little sleepy, right? Maybe, but Father, where would I be if it was not for finding You—in the hands of someone evil or worst. I think it is good to know You are my real Father, although I have never seen You. We can talk to each other anyway about all things. "things like life what I have learned about You, the things I need to learn, how to understand my brothers and sisters and live with them no matter what; loving each other, being in the same world, and experiencing some of the same things to reach total communication with one another (and for a lot of us, that is one of the hardest things to do). Example: Ms. Ross has lots of money. Mr. Bill has about 20 houses. We cannot understand why we have none of this, but we never ask them how they did it or for help to do it. That is, we who are judges of them are feeling bad about ourselves and not knowing why or what is missing in our own lives; not all of us, but a lot of us are this way. Father, as we talk, I guess I am asking You to help me not be afraid to ask for help when I need it. In talking with You, I am grasping a lot of things about me that I did not know about in myself. I understand that there are two sides to every story and that I, most always, would like to hear both sides in that type of situation. You know what I am saying'? When I think about it, I have feeling for the other person's feeling which sometimes can get me in trouble because I will focus on them and not the situation, making bad decisions about what to do. Then, most of the time, it only hurts me. In doing something for someone from my heart, I am as happy about it as I am calm.

Yes, talking with You, Father, also helps me see my faults. Never before have I been so clear in what I must do or how I must be; not should, but must be (that is for me). There are only two places to be—in You or in the world. Though I am in the world, so to speak, I do not have to be of the world, of things in it. I have heard of something that can keep me safe and free from danger and the wrong things of the world. I hear mostly religious people talk about this. They call it the Comforter; something that will keep me meek, hold back my anger, help me be kind and honest in all my affairs, keep me happy in things that I do, help me keep the faith that I have over all, show me the way to righteousness in life and how to handle the bad periods in my life, and give me strength to hold on. I say to You, my Father Whom I have never seen, I feel that is one of the things I need with me at all times, for it will remind me of You—strong, powerful, loving, kind, understanding, and foremost, generous in Your generosity to all who seek You first. Just to know this about You is comforting to me. I would like to have that form of spirit with me now and always. They say it is a spirit, You know, and that you can only receive it through the Lord Jesus Christ. Father, I know You and You alone know Him better than anyone, what I have read of You tells me this. So I am asking You to let Him know that I would like to receive this spirit called the Holy Ghost. For it is said that If I ask in the name of Jesus Christ, it will be given. So, in the name of Jesus Christ, I ask that I receive the Holy Spirit, in the name of Jesus.

Question, my Father. Does one have to be baptized to receive the Holy Spirit or just be a good, God-loving person'? I know two such persons. I do not have to call their names, for once again, You know them. You know that one is very sick and has had a hard time growing up in the world, not understanding a lot of things about himself and not being educated about a lot of things he needed to know. So he choice a way of life he thought he knew and I feel all of that was not his fault. You know, I feel very close to him and I know he needs this Comforter now, more than ever; a warm and kind hand to hold his, for I cannot give him the understanding he is longing to have as he endeavors to find out, "why me?" I do not know myself, but I say to You, my Father, if he could have this right now in his life, it would help him be better and not feel so alone. I know You are with him. Through the Spirit of the Holy Ghost he will know You are with him. So, in as much as I need this Holy Spirit I know all can have it at the same time. If we are in the Lord, and know what he wants us to do and try in our hearts to have a good life, he will comfort us. I feel, Father, that you will will have mercy on us who are innocent of not knowing what to do. I feel I know this person did not know what he was involved in, being a thing of the world. I saw in him kindness and the love of making other people happy with laughter. The little things in him led me to feel he had some of the Creator in him. So Father, I ask You, is this such a bad person to ask the Holy Spirit to keep and be with him now? I ask You, for he only hurt himself. He did not harm anyone that I know about, really. I ask You, Lord, to help him in this time. I give up my right to receive the Holy Ghost for he has not been baptized in the name of Jesus. I sincerely believe he stands innocent of not knowing how he was to live. I only ask that he have some means of being comfortable now, spiritually. Help him, dear Lord.

Father, the other person I love very much and, at times, I really do not care for her behavior and know I can do nothing about that for I cannot change anyone, yet I wish I could. I understand now when people say it is a struggle going on inside of them for it has happened to me. It is like I am not in it but yet something is going on inside. In these times, I find myself saying, "Father, help me". I guess that is where I was suppose to be in that situation—believing You Father Whom I have never seen, but truly love. I feel Your presence in my heart in those times and other times also.

What I cannot quite understand is my bitterness towards her at times, knowing she cannot help herself. I see that because, You know, I have been where she is more or less. I can feel some of her pain, however, we cannot talk about it because she says she is okay; I see it different. I know that instead of being harsh, I should reach out to her, but it is so hard when she is in that other person's attitude. So, once again I need Your help to improve on my part; the part I am suppose to play in this knowing I can do nothing. I have to put it in Your hands, right?

I do admire her for she has great strength and agility. She has a very good perspective on most things outside of herself. Yes, I do believe we have two sides to us, but we are to have the meekness on one side and control on the other. Father, I do see a good person who I believe needs Your touch also in becoming a whole person within the persons of herself. I am here to help her in anyway I can because I know You know about such things and how to handle them. Father, I do not know why I feel I can ask all these things of You when I am suppose to ask my Lord in the name of Jesus, but You know how I am—very particular and choosey about things I feel are personal. I feel very personal about You, my Father Whom I have never seen, because You are my Father; so I automatically ask You for and about things. I do not know of anyone better than You to talk to. So, one thing I can do for the people I love is tell them of You and maybe they will find how easy it is to talk to You about the truth in their hearts_ You will see what has to be done and do it; that is, help us work it out in our lives. Whatever it is that we do not understand or is a problem to us, Father, You know.

SECTION 15:
Being True to Ones Self

Right now, I have a problem that I do not understand—how do I step out on hope? My belief is that my needs will be attended to. I do believe in faith, but I do not know how strong mine is sometimes. If I do as I think I should because of my hope, my wife and others will say I am crazy or something like that. Every time I try to step out on my hope something comes along that makes me see things in a different perspective. You know, Father, something gets in my way to make me take another look at what I really want to do. I always seem to recognize it somehow and not step out on my faith. I do not quite understand that sometimes. I guess it is me not knowing. I know it will be alright and I am determined in my hope, but Father, how do I keep that determination at all times? This lack of determination makes me feel the words in my heart are not as true as they feel coming out of my mouth because I do not put into action those feelings I am speaking of. So, the hope of helping another—he or she or them—by being an example is hard to brag about, except by grace and that means You, my Father Whom I have never seen. Now I feel great confidence, but I know it is in You, Father, and not myself. I need to be in self-reliance also. Yes, my Father, I hear You and know I will not give up for I will get it and the best of You in me will shine forth.

I believe now and understand the saying "only the strong survives". It is referring to the strength of the Lord in me or is what I think is the strength of the Lord. I am glad there are no limitations on prayer or praise, my Father. I am in the need of someone to pray for me without restriction or a final point to which they may pray. I believe in the unity of prayer for it is the harmony of strength for me. Once again, I say to You Father, I am nothing without You in my life in any world; this I know!

I would like to be genuine from this point on. It is all about myself and what I know of my good and bad points; not to be false with myself means a lot to me. I truly want my love for You to show no matter how big or small it may be to me on the outside. I understand the inside a little better than I do the outside for now, but with Your help I will sustain both. You know, there; is something I just realized. I am very easily disheartened about things I believe in or have hope for and this I let other people do to me. I know I must not allow this to happen if I am to get ahead with the things I would like to do—both in the Lord and in the world; first reverence to You, Father, then to the world.

There is not too much I would like out of the things of the world at this point, except to help the children put in my care and other kids of my sisters and brothers at some point. I would just like to have good things for my family. Oh, but the things of the Lord are of no end for I seek all I will be granted by my Father Whom I have never seen. I had not known You in the beginning, but I pray I will in the end of my life here in this world.

Oh Father, if I could just keep talking to You from this moment on, until the end, it sure would be nice. But, I know You have things for me to handle for You, so I will be thankful for this time to talk with You. I am so grateful for so many things I have learned since talking *to You this* little while; not just for material things, but for a lot I have learned about me that is very essential in my life now. Knowing You and learning me makes me, in part, with You; in touch with One so excellent. My Father, it is so important to me to have Your help in being honest with my feelings and open about what is going on *with me*. Sometimes I do not know what is going on with me, so I seek Your *help* by asking on my knees (when I think to do it that way). The *thing is,* I know I need to turn it over to You because being powerless is not so bad when I know who has the power and what can be done by that one. You are the only who has the power to give and take. I understand that life is manageable and I am just not managing it very well; I cannot without Your help, Father. I wish to be in a particular relationship in spirit with You all the time. Regardless of how long it takes me to learn how to relax in my body, the very soul of my being has to respond to Your will, my Father—that I believe with all my heart. I can be obedient to the Lord's words, but I can only do the things I do by Your grace, I have to be in grace with You, my Father Whom I have never seen.

SECTION 16:
Doing the Father's Will/ Responsibility

Father, You hear people say I am too serious about most things and not loose enough (as in having fun), but You know I have had some good times in my heart. I feel the best is yet to come because now I am into letting Your will be done. I already feel the joy of it, okay? So I would say to everyone if you really want to have some fun, then get into the Lord for He has it all on his side. I think of how much fun we all could have if we would only live in peace with each other and let the Lord take over in all things. I say right now Father, take me, all of me to do as You will. I stand in the need of Your will for I have none. I will not fake it to be in Your grace or with You. I know I cannot fool You or myself for we both know the pretense of it. Yes, I do understand that I might go along with somethings until they are set right. I think I need to have patience if I am in hope of things to come; things that are not seen although I see a need for these things in my life right now. As I see it, I can use them now. If I have turned it over to God, then I need not to complain about where I put my trust and that is in You, my Father. There is not anything stronger than the word and grace of the Lord—NONE!

Father, I keep thinking of responsibility and many things come to mind. How do I know when something is not my responsibility? As I am telling You this, I see and hear You saying I first must have good direction in my life and righteousness. In order to have these things, I must know something of You, Father, for You are present in me and can appear to me at anytime. That is what is so good about having You around all the time. I trust You will help me with my responsibilities now that I know to whom I am responsible first in my life. Now I can think about my family because I see that it goes along with responsibility to one's righteousness in self. My Father Whom I have never seen, I now know and understand that I cannot tell my family how to live, but I can discern what is right from what is wrong when I see it in them. I can show the love of caring enough to say this is wrong or that is not right and take on their anger. I see it as things that will keep the family bonded and also show honesty in one another's feelings for the other.

Father, I remember when I was a child, it seemed as if I was the one who always brought the family happiness just by being happy myself. You know, carrying on in fun and always doing something funny or saying funny stuff made them laugh. Now that it is years later, I still see that look of happiness in their eyes that it seems I bring to them when we are together. Lord, You know what I am saying. I think they were hoping I would spring up as "head of the family"; the only one to make it (as people say). I have made it—for I have found You, my Father, and for me that is making it. I believe they are happy that I have found You. As I was growing up, they could see that I missed my father. Thank You, Father, for being around for me to find. Praise God, I see, through You, how much I have missed being close to my family all these years. But because I have found You, Father, I feel I still have a chance to be close to the family. Close to all of those I know and some I can look for or try to reach in some way. Lord, I say to anyone who has a family, get together with them and thank God for them. Love and help one another. Father, You know I love the kids I have in other places. They have families where they are, *but I feel* that all of them (those on their mother's side also) are my family. Lord, You know I truly do. That makes me want to know and understand more about the word, yes the Bible, than anyone. I want to share what I understand; not because I read it, but because You told me so with Your presence as I learned.

First, I need to be constant in my Bible studies and classes at church; more than just on Sunday. I hope to gain that constant desire to go to church more and read of the word and pray on my knees more. My Father, I know I have to do more than talk to You about these things, I should also do something about them; put it in motion. As for the goals I have set, I should work hard on them; have faith and walk with that faith of reaching them and see them to the end as long as it causes no hurt, harm or danger. See them through if I really believe in myself through You. For I know if I stay in You, my self-confidence will always be up to the task at hand.

You know, Father, it seems like I need to have on some kind of war clothes or something at all times to be free to do the things I need or wish to do. I know You understand what I am saying in this regard. No one knows better than You, Father. Right? I thank the Lord there is armor for me. I guess I am going through some process for a lot of things now. It takes a lot of time for some and not so much for others, but one thing for sure—I need You, Father, to be with me right now. I know we (all of Your children) should be in the need of You (and we are); some of us may not know it. Father, I just want to say right here, I love You, Father.

Father, it seems the closer I get to doing the right things in the Lord in all my affairs, the more something tries to stop me. Without You there and in faith that You are there for me, I will not handle it. For I have seen the faces of some of my sisters and brothers who, as the Holy Spirit and I, want the same thing; I know that is the look of being in God. I have had that feeling in me and know there is nothing better, nothing; but, it did not last and I have to have it back for the rest of my life to have life and share it with others. I want to help those who have no faith to know how to have faith in the Lord in the name of Jesus and to give praise. Thank You, Lord!

I just want to say thank You, my Father Whom I have never seen. I am thankful for each *day I am able to see* although I may not get up being happy. I do not know why not, but thank the Lord. I need to let him know that each day, now at least I know to say thank You, Lord and make it a habit everyday I am blessed to see. For in doing so, all things can be better for me and of me—any pain or hurt, unhappiness; just any problem can be alleviated if endured in Christ Jesus.

Father, help me alter all things that will not keep me in this close relationship with You. Father, help me come out of my heart and into the light with the things I know are right. Open my ears so I may hear the words You are speaking to me. I hope to get on *with the things about You* and Your teachings for me to return to the Lord when I am done down here. Help me put God first in my life and in the light of day. I believe there is light in the darkness. If I have the light of God, it will shine any place and anytime. For the light within will shine through; this I believe. But how, my Father, do I get this light in my heart to come forth without seeming to be acting "holier than Thou", as people say. I wish not to hurt anyone's feelings in my actions about our relationship or is this concern the wrong thing to be worried about? Or, should I just allow my heart and faith in the Lord to guide me? What I am saying is that I want to help people who do not know the Lord like I do. But if they feel that I think I am so Holy, they may not want or let me help them, You know. Oh yes, I know all I can do is plant the seed and turn it over to

You. You are right, Father, as always. Father, I have this thought about role models. We hear people say that kids mostly need role models to look up to, to follow; particularly children with no dad in the home. My thought is that the mother or person in charge of that child or young person should teach him/her that the only role model really needed is the Lord. Who better then He is the perfect role model? What do they think is His purpose? I believe a role model should be someone who, first of all, has love to give, has strength, is powerful, unblemished, and intelligent. Also, one who can invoke divine favor. To me, this is the only real meaning of role model and You, my Father Whom I have never seen, are all of these things and much more. So, again, who is more adequate than He One who will never let me down or leave? One who can surpass any problem that will arise. Yes, and I speak just for me, You are my hero and role model. I understand I am not You and can never be You, but I can follow in Your path for You are showing me the right way by leaving Your word for me to learn. I understand that being made in Your image means good is already within me, so the role model is there also. But first, I must have someone show me where to start looking. That is where we who are here to be in charge of the children come in. We must remember that we are all Your children.

Father, I now can see that I would have everything I want if had grown up knowing You are in me and all things come by You. Well, You know as well as I that it is not too late. If I get into You, all these things will still be; this I believe. Now that I have elected to follow the path of salvation, I will do my best to stay; staying in line with that which I have chosen. I believe we are subjected to the over-and-over things of the world so we can realize that God is always right; when we were created He knew it could be done right. We must learn how to live as He has said. We have all the tools to do this—the death, burial, and resurrection of our Lord and Savior Jesus Christ was for the remission of our sins; all of these we have along with the protection from evil.

Father, I see that we ourselves cause You to make a choice as to when "enough is enough" and when You will have to choose for some of us to go on. I understand, Father, that there should not be fear in doing what I feel is right for me and have faith in that. I have You to guide me. Now that I think about it, I should have known that someone who loves His children as You, would have an open way for them to get to Him and communicate at anytime. Father, why did I not think of that before now? Well, now I know where You are. You can expect me to be talking to You often, okay?

I find it to be so satisfying to talk with You; there is so much joy and peace and I sure hope this will continue for I long to know more of You and the Spirit of You, my Father. Whatever it is I can do, use me, okay? Just call me and I will come running to You, my Father Whom I have never seen. You know I do not talk very much, but I seem to be doing a lot of it now. I guess when you find one you have been looking for for some time, there are a lot of thing.; to be said and asked about.

SECTION 17:
Feelings

I was so excited I forgot to ask how are You? Dumb question, right? It was a thought in my heart; You know what I am feeling. Oh yes, while I am on feelings again, remember when I was singing and I hit a very high and good note which I felt down inside me? I cannot describe it; all I know is that it was a very good and strange happening. Anyway, that is how I felt praising the Lord in church Sunday; something ran through me. What was that, Father? Sometimes I get that feeling when I just know something good is going to happen. It is very strange sometimes, but I hope I keep having those good feelings and also remorse when I am wrong for I believe they work together in some way. As good works against evil, so does regret work against guilt. I believe I do not have the explanation for this, but You do. I believe when it is time, there will be an answer from You. I will keep making an effort to acquire all of the knowledge You have already left for us.

You know what I have noticed? Most of us need a lot of attention or seem to want it, for some reason. We look for it in each other and not in the creature who is here; yes, here to be attentive to us in the same way one would look after a child in ones care, I believe, Father. Yes, now I understand and realize why Marcus wants so much attention and gets bored when there is nothing for him to do. I think he feels the contents of what he first felt as a small baby is removed. That loving feeling, so to speak, is gone at those times and may be for a lot of us. That happens and we do not know why at the time. All we know is that we feel a need to do something and sometimes that can be bad. You know what I mean?

I have felt empty in the past, Father, and You know I have; but now that I have found You as a friend and Savior, there is no more emptiness. I can tell You anything at anytime in my life, good or bad feelings or just things in general. You will understand, love, and help me get better. Sometimes just talking makes it all better, but I do say that those of us who do not know who to talk to should have someone with the knowledge of God to talk with. Carrying around bad feelings does not help; there is no place for them in you and that is the way I felt. You, Father, have said I can be happy, joyful and free. I just ask in the name of Jesus Christ and I shall receive. Thank You, Lord.

Father, I know if a lot of people could hear me now they would probably say I am full of stuff, You know, but I believe You know that in my heart I am trying to put You first and not the things of the world. They are already mine and You in my life mean more than all those things now that I know the only true love and where it lies for me. When I cannot find the words to express the way I feel about You in my life, I will just say, "'Thank You, Jesus". You are out of the highest orders of all things here and therein (here in my heart and there in the world). I compensate this debt the only way I know how and that is here am I; take me as I am—I owe You so much for as long as I live, my Father. Bless Your Holy name, Jesus.

My Father, I am looking forward to You coming by here. When You will, stop by here. Now I understand that as the Priest of the fruits, You allured me to plant. I am that seed's clergyman; therefore, it is up to me to conduct and minister first to those offsprings the teaching of the word. That is what I believe to be right because I am given the capability through You to do this. I believe once given this power, it is never too late to use it for it will not be taken back. All I have to do is remember that I have it, from whom I obtained this gift and know that it is confirmed in the name of Jesus, the Son of my Father Whom I have never seen. I would like to acquire patience and meekness with those that I do not understand at times or the children when they are not acting as I think they should. Just to be able to show compassion at those times is what I need to know and feel I must do, okay?

My Father, I am experiencing how it must feel to have to let one of your children go when you love them so. Regardless of the reason, something happens inside; well, for us humans anyway. But, I feel You can have these feelings also in some instances since You are real (my opinion, of course). Father, I just hope (for the sake of those of Your children who do not know You or have not found You) that it is alright for me to help them. I have Your permission? Yes? Good? I know some of them know how to get in touch but will not, as though You have done something to them and the life they have. That is their own choice and will. Lord, I pray that You will give me the strength to resist my own will and the Devil's. Oh Father, thank You for the messages You left for me. For if I had not found them, I would not have found You.

Thank You, Lord. I am so thankful that You let whatever it was down inside me You were around somewhere and that You are still there just like a little voice at times telling me things. I am learning that voice so I will not make a mistake in whose it is.

I guess knowing the things that are in me are very important and significant to what I can and may act out in my daily life. I need that guidance of truth to be there in me; the fear of God so to speak. Father, You know what I am saying, fear of not doing what I know is right each day. Right now I am eating too much and I know I need to do something about this daily because my heart needs to be clean in order to work properly in its feelings. My spirit is telling me that You will be turning Your attention to another matter in a few minutes but for me not to fear, for You can do all things at the same time so I can keep on talking. But I will not because I have to go and give out the good news that I have found You. How happy I am that I could talk to You and can at anytime I want and need to my Father Whom I have never seen!

Now, I know You love me for I have felt Your very words of that feeling. Oh, Father You do love me. I am so blessed to have this love of all loves. Praise the Lord! It is no way that You will not hear from me again soon. Even now, before I am gone, I cannot wait to get back to talk to You just for a little while. As You know, I am getting ready to move again, but this time I know it will be different for me for I have grown since talking with You. You have shown me how to be head of my household, how to be helpful in my own life, and how to live Holy and with the Spirit that is in me—the foundation of my very purpose. Again, I just want to say, "'Thank You, Lord".

I do understand that I must have a willing mind and heart to go through whatever it takes to let the Lord do His will and believe that His will for me also becomes my will for me through Him. That means that I have to learn what His will is for me by praying and listening to His words with my heart and the voice within me; asking for His help as I need it everyday. I know I need Jesus in my life every hour of everyday. I do not know about you, but no matter what, I need Him. Life without You, Father, is hopeless and I do not want to live without You in it. I love Jesus Christ and my Lord, God too for They are in me and I cannot denounce that strange feeling of constant presence and knowing it has something to do with all that goes on inside me (the voice and all).

Father, there are so many things I have not seen in my life yet, but I will try to learn the Word and the way to obedience. I believe the best days of my life here are about to come and I know that is only by Your means. Bless You, my Father, for I can use a change right about now. Yes, I will wait on my blessings. Thank You, Lord.

I hear people say that the last days are here and soon Jesus will be back. Who, but You, knows for sure how close or far off You are? For me, that is kind of scary because I am not ready and I know this, but I am trying to get ready through praying and giving praise to the Lord as I learn about the Word and what it means to me. Hallelujah! I am stepping out in faith that I have help from You on this journey, my Father, for I do not know how to do it alone. Knowing Your love for me lets me see that I will never be alone as long as I am in You, You will show up in me. That accompanied by other things in me makes everything alright, I do believe this.

Father, as I said earlier, I can see and feel all the things You are showing me to be true and clear as to how they will be for me and the children of Your choice. The only way we can truly come into You is by complying with Your Words. I now understand that it is for the children now in our care that I must learn how to live Holy and in the will of the lord that they may feel and see the miracle of You, my Father Whom I have never seen. If they know You through learning from the message of the Word You have left for us to use for the purpose of teaching, the children, as well as ourselves, will learn the good news that Jesus is alive, alive, alive! Father, as I talk to You of how I wish I had my life in order in Your sight, I now know how it feels not to owe any man a thing and be thankful that I can owe one that will accept me as payment for all He has done and for all I have and will be given. "Thank You, Lord'. I want to pay my tithes and offerings because You are worthy and I know that is a way of showing thanksgiving to You from my heart if, in fact, I am actually thankful to You. I know this will be a problem for me because I put other things first most of the time. But I believe now that I am serious, I can and will do it in all honesty for I know it is right in the Lord. All things can be done if I believe in the Lord, right Father?

Father, I pray that when I am through talking with You, I will have this same spiritual feeling and understanding to keep me in You as I am today. Right now, only You and I know how I feel. You know Father, it just came to me that I have received this feeling because of You.

I feel parents should not tell a child growing up that he or she is spoiled. The child will believe he/she is damaged and unfit if that is constantly said, not knowing what the words mean but knowing that it gives them a bad feeling I know; that is the way it made me feel until now. I now know I am a good person, but look how long it took for me to realize that. If it were not for You, I *may* still *have* that thought inside me. That is just how I felt, but I am convinced I now can cope with this.

One reason I believe we should teach the children is because they are special to the real Father and He loves them. No matter what l say, find Him and you will find Eternal peace and joy *with* happiness. But, I do believe you have to make some kind of covenant with Your Father. If you are to trust in Him and His love, then He should have some way of letting You commit yourself to Him. I believe if you are serious about wanting to do this, then you will have the right fear of God in you to let you be true to your pledge and the relationship with Him. For me, that means letting Him carry me through things and having the faith that He is going through them with me. That means it is going to be okay. For You, I can and do put myself through things and He will lets me go through them to see what I will do or how I will handle them. I know the things I put myself through are different from those the Lord allures me to undergo. He is there to help me in either case.

SECTION 18:
Summary

Father, some of these things I might have said already, but I feel the need to reiterate or remind myself of the things that will help it work for me. You know, Father, I am just feeling so much better now. I know I am about to go for now, but it is as if I have been talking to more than one intelligence here inside me. I hear and feel a force greater than I have ever felt before. I feel so much of God in me, Lord and Jesus Christ in You, my Father Whom I have never seen, that You and my Father have to be the same—glory be to You. Hallelujah! I know this is true for I feel it like I know. I know and that feels so good; better than anything I have felt at anytime. I praise You and I love *You*, Lord, with all that is in me. You are one and I will *show* all *the* people I love that I really love them so they will know this no matter what.

I feel very bad that I have a lot of love in me that has not come out I believe that very love can help someone and if only for a moment, make that life a little brighter—the love all of us have in us to make life shine. Yes, we do have it, all of us.

Now that I know the light is in me, I need help to get it to shine. I know that only You, my Father Whom I have never seen, can do this for me. What You do for me, You will do for another. This I know for it was a miracle I found You, but the real miracle is the love of You to let me find You—to know someone I have never seen loves me more than I could ever love myself. I will not stay away for long. I will always be looking forward to seeing You in person and being with You, Father. I am so glad to have met You.

Love,
Your Son

978-0-595-48163-7
0-595-48163-9

Printed in the United States
121567LV00003B/44/P